Recession Buster: 10 steps to managing your household budget

(A little at a time)

Tokie Laotan-Brown

Recession Buster: 10 steps to managing your household budget
(A little at a time)

Copyright © 2013 by Tokie Laotan-Brown

All rights reserved. No part of this book may be reproduced or transmitted in any form or by any means without written permission from the author.

ISBN-13: 978-1492184331

Printed in USA.

Dedication

To my wonderful family: Laotan, Eribo and Brown.

Table of Contents

Preface 5
Introduction 6
STEP 1: Get Organized! 7
STEP 2: Assess your situation 10
STEP 3: Work out your budget 15
STEP 4: Debt reduction 20
STEP 5: Dealing with debt 25
STEP 6: Managing payments 27
STEP 7: Evaluating budgets regularly 32
STEP 8: Setting financial goals 34
STEP 9: Dealing with a spendthrift partner 35
STEP 10: Holding everyone accountable 39
Conclusion 40

Preface

This book will not teach you how to invest your money but rather on how to get the most out of the current amount of money that comes in to the household.

I will not focus on how to get rich fast or any wall-street strategies but teach you how to make good use of pennies or cents that gets overlooked within the current budget of household finances.

The emphasis of this book will be to look at outgoings and how to reduce bill payouts with consistent discipline.

Using simple mathematical calculations, managing household budgets on a weekly or monthly basis will help in reducing the stress of anticipating bill pay outs as they roll in.

Introduction

The reason behind this book is to acknowledge the fact that, there is a recession and majority of the people around the world are being squeezed with numerous outgoings. I understand the squeeze and I have come to understand the math behind household budgeting without the added stress.

I have helped a lot of my friends in coping with the dreaded concept of household budgeting and making sure that being bullied by bill operators does not become a weekly or monthly chore.

This book will lay down 10 simple steps to a structured way of dealing with the current recession and how to use your actual finances that are incoming to elevate and dictate to bill operators on how you will like to pay your own bills.

When I give a one on one consultation, the main question I am asked is, *"How do I cope when suddenly a bill comes from nowhere?"*

I usually answer by saying, *"That is why you prepare by putting money aside and calling it miscellaneous"*. This way you feel you are saving by default.

"This is what helps you get out of sticky situations!"

STEP 1
Get Organized!

This is the most difficult of the steps, once this is sorted, budgeting will then become easier to manage.

A plan of action needs to be put into place with the money coming in (any income into the household finances) and the money going out or expenditure (any money being used to pay for bills within the household). Your budget needs to show that the outgoings are less or equal to what is coming in.

Your budget is supposed to help you see how much money comes in and how much goes out. It will also show where you are spending too much and what is consuming the most money.

How frequently some monies come in and the amount that is generated, obviously this will influence how the money is spent in the household.

This will help with planning for bills as well as unexpected expenses. It is important for everyone within a household that has an income and has bills to pay- **to make a budget!** If you receive your income weekly, then do a weekly budget. If you receive your income monthly, then do a budget monthly. The same for bi-weekly incomes.

If your income is received in spirals- (for example, people that have multiple incomes by working numerous jobs) - then the budget can be organized around the incomes. I will be giving specific examples in the book later on. Also taxes are different all over the world. Depending on culture, some households look after their elderly relatives and/or siblings. All these expenses need to be added to the outgoings.

Take out a notebook and a pen/pencil.

Add up all the income that comes into the household and note when they come in and the frequency.

You will need to make sure that all incomes are calculated after tax and levies depending on your country's laws. Include overtime incomes when you receive it. Make sure that tax payments have been deducted before adding it to the income column of your note book. Include all tax relief, allowances when you receive it. Remember, you will be doing your budget; weekly, bi-weekly or monthly as you receive monies. It is very important that you do a budget as money comes into the household.

You will have your actual budget plan, this you do as you receive income and your forecast plan based on monies you expect to have as the months progress with allowances to adjust when the need arises.

Any social welfare benefits, child benefits, spousal allowance, child maintenance payments need to be included as income. It is also important to include contributions from other people who live in your household, such as adult children, partners or siblings. Making sure that any non-dependant living in the house is paying enough towards the household expenses.

I will not be addressing assets in this particular book as I want to focus on actual monies that come into a household. These days it has become increasingly difficult to work out assets for many households since the recession has devalued equity on many owner-occupier homes.

For Example: Lucy works as a cashier in a local store and earns 1,100 Euros after tax and levies have been deducted. She also has 2 kids and gets a child benefit of 60 Euros a week from the government. In addition, as a single parent she receives child maintenance payments of 800 Euros a month. See chart below

Income	**Frequency**	**Amount** Euros

Salary	Monthly	1100
Child Benefit	Weekly	60 X 4
Maintenance payments	Monthly	800
Total		2140

Lucy's total income that she receives in a month from various sources is 2,140 Euros. This total excludes taxes, levies, contributions and pension schemes. These are all taken out before she receives her salary. For other countries, it might be different. I am using Ireland, where I reside as an example. You might have to pay your taxes and levies after you have received your paycheck. So check and be sure that all taxes and contributions have been paid for.

STEP 2
Assess your situation

Assess your outgoings, work out with your family how much money you need to spend each week on basic living expenses. Start a weekly spending journal. Keep track of all your spending, do this over a 2 month period. This process will help you see where your money is really going.

It can also help with tracking monies spent on eating out, shopping on impulse and various bits and bobs that you pick randomly.....like the bottle of sodas, sweets etc. Impulse buying is the biggest threat to scheduled budgets!

Do a Scale of Preference when assessing your budget: List your most important bills at the top and your secondary bills at the bottom of the same list. Make a list of those you will need to contact to explain a payment plan on another page.

Now back to looking at the financial outgoings for your family; the most important bills that you have to take into consideration always will be bills that provide for your shelter, feeding and heating (in cold climates).

Your rent or mortgage is another important bill and needs to take priority on your Scale of Preference, alongside feeding. They make the two largest chucks of bills that any household will incur. Heating bills are the next in line depending on which region you reside in.

Now this format will be helpful for people living from paycheck to paycheck, people finding it difficult to plan their bills around their daily activities.
The bill list is a good way to start.

- Mortgage or rent
- Food and groceries
- Electricity, heating and air conditioning expenses
- Property taxes

- Insurance costs
- Savings and investment contributions
- Home maintenance costs
- Heating and air conditioning expenses
- Utilities, such as electricity, water, sewer, trash pick up
- Medical expenses, such as medical bills, prescriptions, hospital parking
- Child care and child support expenses
- Vehicle expenses
- Loans
- Credit cards
- Clothing
- Memberships
- Personal care
- Entertainment, recreation and hobby expenses

As I mentioned above, figure out what bills need to be addressed ASAP. Write to your creditors, stating that you are assessing your finances and will get back to them on how much you can afford to pay either weekly or monthly, depending on the frequency of your income.

Let's refresh, identify your bills, and make sure they are in your name. Make sure you have contacted creditors in writing to let them know you are assessing your finances and will get back to them to let them know how much. During this assessment process, also consider the possibility of future emergencies and how you can be prepared. If you identify financial concerns, short-term and long-term planning along with saving and spending reductions will be addressed.

For example Tunde has just received a statement on the 22nd of November 2012. He had just incurred a bill of 320 Euros on his electricity bill that has been added to an outstanding bill of 128 Euros from his last bill dated the 15th of August 2012. The total bill is now 448 Euros. His mortgage is 1, 200 Euros every month. Tunde lives with his wife and three sons, one of which works as a bank clerk. The other two sons are still in college. He has received three notices from his mortgage lender and a few notices from various other creditors and is running short of money to pay for the rising costs of bills within the household. He will need to assess his financial status.

PRIMARY BILLS WITH TOP PRIORITY				
Primary Bill	**Debt Total**	**Arrears**	**Frequency**	**Note**
Mortgage	120,876	2,400	Monthly	Letter
Electricity	448	128	Bi-Monthly	Letter
Food/Groceries	360	-	Bi weekly	Renegotiate
Property taxes	480	-	Yearly	Ok
Personal Insurance/Pension	256	-	Monthly	Ok
Education (Kids)	36,000	-	Yearly	Ok

It is alluring to list a lot of categories, but don't go overboard. If you are writing it in a notebook, just use basic categories. If you're using excel, you can create more, as you need them.

SECONDARY BILLS				
Secondary Bill	**Debt Total**	**Arrears**	**Frequency**	**Note**
Household Supplies	150	-	Bi Yearly	Ok
Car Expenses	480	80 (Policy)	Monthly	Letter
Credit cards/Loans	1,800	560	Monthly	Letter
Memberships	400	-	Yearly	Renegotiate
Hobbies	120	-	Yearly	Ok
Clothing	300	-	4/ yearly	Ok
Dining out	250	-	Occasionally	Ok
Savings	200	-	Occasionally	Ok

After you have assessed your financial situation, it is time to prepare a letter to your creditor. Remember to make note of how many letters you are writing, in Tunde's case, he will be writing 4 letters. Take note of who you are writing to, the correct address (call to make sure), and the correct reference number of your account with the creditor. Once the letter has been written, keep a copy for your files.

Here is an example of a letter Tunde will be writing to his creditor:

36, Rosalene Road
Westbrook
London

23rd of November 2012

Re Account Ref: XXX123564
Dear Sir/Madam,

I am writing in regards to the above reference account detail. Due to current financial difficulties, I am currently assessing my financial obligations.

I will be contacting you with a detailed statement on how I will be paying off my current debt, while taking into account my living expenses and commitments.

I will also like to take this opportunity to request a suspension to any debt collection orders or charges that are being incurred due to late payments.
I will forward my payment statement in 2 weeks.

Thanks for your continued understanding.

Yours Sincerely,
Tunde Obadele.

Debt payoff - Paying off any kinds of debt should be a high priority. It will free up your income for future opportunities when you are not burdened with the monthly payments and interest.

Home - Rent or mortgage payment, insurance, property taxes. You could even include home repairs and furnishings in this budget category.

Utilities – Monthly bills for water, electricity, gas, phone, internet, cable.

Car expenses – Car payments, gas, insurance, repairs, motor tax, inspection.

Healthcare – Doctor/Dental visits and prescriptions.

Food – Groceries and toiletries.

Personal – Clothing, dinning out etc.

One off items – Set aside money each month for any one off items before buying them.

Miscellaneous – Save for unexpected events, this helps you stick to your budget.

Tithes and giving – Remember I wrote about cultural responsibilities in step 1, well, that's where money to look after elderly relatives or/and siblings goes.

STEP 3
WORK OUT YOUR BUDGET

A household budget is a good way of addressing debt problems and managing your home. Step 1 helped with working out how much comes into the home and step 2 assessed the amount that goes out of the home in relation to bills and costs.

This is important because it helps the householders see how much money is coming in and how much is going out. Figure out how much is left and work out a financial commitment to creditors. Plan future spending and separate living needs from credit commitments.

At step 3, you will have figured out the actual total income the household earns either on a weekly or monthly basis. Best to stick to one, most people opt for a monthly schedule. You will also have figured out the total actual payments made out for bills and costs: yearly, monthly or weekly. Pick a convenient schedule that makes the budget easier to handle.

For most utility bills, you might either receive them on a monthly or bi monthly basis. Check your last bill; multiply it by 6 to get a yearly amount, if you receive bi-monthly. If your budget is going to be planned on a weekly basis, divide the yearly amount by 52 weeks to get a weekly amount for your budget plans. If it is for a monthly budget, divide the yearly amount by 12. For a more accurate weekly or monthly average, contact your utility supplier and request a statement of consumption from last year and divide by 52 for a weekly plan and 12 for a monthly plan.

Prepare a Household Budget Plan	Keep in mind that your budget does not have to be complicated as long as it meets your needs. If you do not want to set up your own budget format, there are many styles of budget worksheets available online as well as in various financial planning books to help you itemize and record your financial
<ul><li>List of all income sources that are available to you, including salary or wages from employment, social welfare benefits,</li></ul>	

- retirement income, investment income, and money gained through an inheritance or trust.
- Budget categories that reflect your total monthly expenses.
- Fixed expenses or those that do not vary much each month, including mortgage or rent costs, loan repayments, insurance policy, property taxes, and income taxes.
- Variable expenses or those that vary every month, including food, dental and medical expenses, maintenance and repairs of home and cars, home utilities and transportation expenses.
- An amount of money that will be used for savings or investments in your budget. Even if it is a very small amount, you will be taking a step towards building savings for your future.
- Money to be used for clothing, travel, entertainment and hobbies. During this process, pay attention to things for which you spend money but may

information.

Use the amount of your net (take-home) income for your budgeting and not your gross (before taxes) income amount.

Compare your total net monthly income to your total monthly expenses to identify your cash flow status.

If you are self-employed, remember to include quarterly estimated tax payments.

Look at your budget in terms of both monthly and yearly spending patterns. For example, seasonal heating or cooling expenses may put extra strain on your budget during certain times of the year.

Consider your budget as an itemized prediction of income and expenses for a specified period.

Decide whether you want or need to change spending habits. If you have enough income to meet required expenses, your budget may still help you see ways that you can redirect spending priorities.

Keep in mind the following percentage amounts that are generally recommended for a personal spending plan:

not need, such as specialty coffee beverages, dining out and books. • Investment income to build security for your future. For example; savings, retirement plans, the purchase of real property and other ways to invest.	• Housing and debt – 35% • Utilities- 20% • Household costs – 24% • Savings – 15% • Insurance – 4% • Transportation – 2% Keep track of bank accounts, savings, credit card and other investment account information and activity. A financial software may be a useful tool for this. Some credit card companies offer a year-end summary of your card expenses. This is another way to track where you spent money throughout the past year.

The amounts that you think you can afford will go in an **"Amounts Column"**. During the month as you go through your receipts, you will update your budget with the **"Actual Amounts"** in the second column. **It is important to note that, everyone's budget is different and you will need to consider your own household's outgoings and the amount you may budget for certain areas will depend on your circumstances. For instance: special diet, health circumstances, use of public transportation or preference for sporting activities or hobbies. So the figures you assign to your budget needs to reflect in your household budget. Extended family commitments are normal for ethnic households living in the diaspora, these needs to be reflected in your budget also. If this is not reflected in the plan, it can make it difficult to stick to a long- term plan and lead into more debt related issues. If you are spending more than your income, then reduce your spending or increase your income by finding extra jobs, check for entitlements, or check for tax refunds if applicable.**

It is also important to check that you are spreading out repayments diligently; weekly, bi-weekly or monthly depending on your budgeting plan. As noted earlier, analyze your outgoings and find out if you can cut down on spending, take care not to cut down on basics such as food, heating/electricity, unless there is excessive spending in these areas.

As you go through your notes, you will notice payments you can't do without, like your rent or mortgage, unless you will consider relocation or changing mortgage lenders for a cheaper option.
Maybe economize on utility bills like telephone, cable or Internet deals. By keeping a daily grocery-shopping journal, you might be able to notice patterns and excesses.

Household social activities might have to have a timetable pattern, so as to reduce excessive spending or impulsive dining out. You might also find out that through budget planning that shopping around for goods and services can help with financial savings.

For bills that vary by a couple of Euros every month, like the water bill, you will need to plan by rounding up a few Euros from the average amount. The electric bill is always higher in the winter depending on what you use for heating, so you could budget for the higher amount, or request average billing. You can always adjust your budget for seasonal changes.

- You can include toiletries with the groceries or have a household supplies category.

- Your grocery bills can vary from one month to the next since it depends on whether you like to stock up. You can still use an average amount. In the following months you should be able to spend less on food so it will balance out.

- It will make sense to plan for one off items by saving for it. You are mostly limited by how much available income you still have after other expenses. Think ahead how much you plan to spend on moments like, Christmas and/or home upgrades in the following year.

- For bills you only pay occasionally, you can set the money aside in advance. Consider having a monthly share automatically drafted into one or more savings accounts. You want to have the money ready before you need it.

- What if the expenses are more than the income? It's time to trim, drastically if needed. A serious look at needs versus wants is hard but necessary.

A written household plan helps identify and clarify goals, increase income, reduce debt and manage your finances. Your plan does not need to be complicated. However, a household plan does need to be monitored and re-evaluated on a regular basis. If you are not able to meet your original management goals, you can always change your plan or adjust your goals. The important thing is to start taking steps now to get your finances under control.

STEP 4
Debt reduction

A good household plan provides guidance for savings and debt reduction. You may find that a change in spending habits can quickly increase savings so that you are able to reduce your debt level. Some people may also want to evaluate whether taking a better paying job or adding a part-time job would be a good idea.

When assigning monies for the expenses columns, it is always a good idea to work on the most pressing debts. Debts that cause red alert beeps to go off in your head. Those ones that cause you to panic, well, you know the one. Mortgage/rent payments are the singular most important debts we incur. Planning for debt reduction will require diligent and consistent payment plans. I repeat CONSISTENT payment plans.

Once it has been ascertained that bill arrears have been noted in step 2 and a letter to a creditor stating that an assessment is taking place. It is very important that a follow up letter is sent with an included payment plan procedure. To support the offer of a payment plan, try to pay the current bill before the next one arrives.

Your payment plan offer must include a current payment plan and an offer off the arrears. As you await an approval to proceed, begin your payment immediately. Do not offer more than what you can afford, that is what managing a budget is all about. Do not allow any intimidation to throw you off balance.

PRIMARY BILLS WITH TOP PRIORITY				
Primary Bill	**Debt Total**	**Arrears**	**Frequency**	**Note**
Mortgage	120,876	2,400	Monthly	2 Letters sent
Electricity	448	128	Bi-Monthly	2 Letters sent

Taking Tunde's household budget example from step two, lets break it down further. He pays 1,200 Euros monthly and now has an arrears of 2,400 Euros, this indicates that he owes 2 months on his mortgage. He has also indicated on his table that 2 letters concerning this debt has been sent. The same was noted for the electricity bill. The above table shows also that this is his most important bills for the household. Let us assume that his income is 3,400 Euros a month.

TUNDE'S HOUSEHOLD BUDGET				
Monthly Income	3,400			
Important Debt	Actual Payment	Arrears	Payment plan	No. of Months for payment
Mortgage	1,200	2,400	180	14 months
Electricity	320	128	20	7 months
Property taxes	480			
Personal insurance/pension	256			
TOTAL	2,256			
Balance	1,144			

Tunde has decided to assign 200 Euros of his balance towards his important bill arrears and will be done with his mortgage arrears in 14 months. He will be adding an extra 180 Euros every month to his current mortgage bill, thereby paying a 1,380 every month until his arrears have been cleared. He will be applying the same principle to his electricity bill. This way, he has 944 Euros for his other bill commitments and savings. In a year and 2 months, he can assign the 200 Euros towards savings or divide up towards other commitment depending on his budget.

Once you have figured out your primary and important debts, as well as debts that are heading towards fines or court cases. The left over bills after groceries have been assigned monies will be your secondary debts. Generally, you will have assigned a monthly or weekly payment plan according to monies available.

For example, Hiromi and his wife Jiaying, have 55 Euros to divide between 4 creditors.

The total budget they have assigned to the 4 creditors to pay off their debt is a total of 55 Euros.

They owe: Credit cards a total of 2,300 Euros
           Household appliances 4,100 Euros
           Bank loan 1450 Euros
           Online shopping catalogue 870 Euros
Total: 8,720 Euros

For their credit cards it will be 2300 X 55 Euros = 126500
                126500/8720 Euros = **14.50 Euros**
For their household appliances, 4100 X 55 Euros = 225500
                225500/8720 Euros = **25.87 Euros**
For their Bank loan, 1450 X 55 Euros = 79750
                79750/8720 Euros = **9.15 Euros**
Online shopping catalogue, 870 X 55 Euros = 47850
                47850/8720 Euros = **5.48 Euros**

Total secondary offer: 14.50 + 25.87 + 9.15 + 5.48 = 55 Euros

It is also advisable to find out about debt charges that will be incurred on your account while you are trying to sort out your household payments.

If you realize that there is no money left after your monies have been assigned to various creditors and you still have some creditors left to pay. Send a letter stating you have no money left and send a plan statement, showing payments to other creditors and when it will be convenient to start their own payment plan. In Tunde's plan, he will be finishing his mortgage arrears in 14 months and his electrical bill in 7 months. So this type of payment plan schedule can accompany a creditor letter showing an indication that after 7 months, the 20 Euros that was set aside to pay off the electricity bill can be used to offset a particular secondary arrears or bill. This sort of agreement can also be used to negotiate a holiday break with the particular creditor. With consistency and making sure at the appointed date a payment is made, this will elevate any unnecessary stress arising from constant creditor call outs or letters.

After paying off any outstanding debts, any monies left over should go into savings and investments instead of thinking of it as "free spending money." Why? Putting extra money away during months of excess will carry you through the tough times. Unless you want to always have panic attacks each time you are faced with impeding bill crisis, feast or famine. Setting money aside when there is extra will give you a sense of stability and peace. Besides, social activities, dinning out and entertainment have already been included in your budget. You do not have to deprive yourself.

Reducing household bills can be divided amongst non-dependant occupants within the household. Make sure every non-dependant individual with a personal debt within the household (with signatories to any debt) has a plan to reducing the debt they owe.

Now, this next part is crucial to the success of debt reduction in a household bill management plan. In the case where there is more than one non-dependant individual in a household, there are two options that can either mar or make a successful household budget plan.

Option one: This is where everyone in the household is ready and willing to help in the plans to reduce the debt in the household. Consistency is the key here as well as cooperation.

Option two: This is where cooperation is a problem and it is actually stressful to try to plan long term goals that will be beneficial to the household, when you are not getting the full cooperation of the entire household. In this option, it is only the person who signs a credit agreement that is responsible for the debt.

A husband and wife are not responsible for each other's debt unless they both sign the agreement. The same for non-dependant individuals residing in the home. If an agreement is jointly taken out by a number of non-dependant individuals, then you are all jointly responsible for the whole debt, not just part of it. This must be emphasized when writing creditors in relation to debt reduction payment plans. Credit agreements need to be double-checked and all parties involved notified.

Check your payment plan agreement to find out if you are also paying for payment protection insurance. This protection cover helps with repayments, when you are unable to work due to accidents, sick or can't work. Some policies might include redundancies. Always check policies! Some creditors might refuse any offer you might present to them. But the idea is to still pay whatever you CAN afford according to your budget plans. As long as you are showing consistency, you will be fine.

Make sure even though you are paying off your debts, that you cross check with your creditor to find out if you are paying interest. Find out if interest rates will be frozen, if not still pay off your debts according to plan, the only difference might be that the number of months/weeks it might take to finish off the debt might be a little longer.
If some other creditors have taken your offer and sent letters stating this, use it to persuade other creditors to accept.

STEP 5
Dealing with debt

Dealing with debt, on a scale of preference starts with your most important and immediate debt.

Begin by making an offer after careful consideration of all you incomings and outgoings.

List the amount of letters that will be written, this will be obvious after you have compiled all your incomes and expenditures for the household.

Prepare a letter with a well organized financial statement to your creditor.

- Include your account details, or reference number of the bill in relation to the debt.
- Explain the reason for the arrears, for example separation, illness, redundancy etc
- Prepare a statement showing when payments will begin, how much you can afford to pay and how long you will be paying. Indicate start date and finish dates. State if the payments will be done on a weekly, bi-weekly or monthly schedule.
- Request a freeze on charges or interest rates.

Offer Accepted

If your offer has been accepted, in writing, send a letter thanking the creditor for their cooperation and let them know what mode of payment you will be using.

Non Acceptance of an offer

If your letter has not being accepted, write back stating that other creditors have been cooperative and enclose a copy of the letters received from other creditors. Also request that they reconsider the offer and inform them about your mode of payment. Start payments immediately based on the offer made and inform them that payments have commenced. If they refuse to freeze charges or interest, write them that, it will be difficult to finish off the debt on time.

If the creditor is insisting that they will go to court, gather all correspondence between you and the creditor. Budget plans and other correspondence with other creditors. Include any payments ongoing, making sure you have been consistent with payments and tender all as evidence in court. As long as you are consistent with payments, the outcome of the court order will reflect on what you have tendered.

The same can be done for secondary debts as well.

In many cases, an effective debt management strategy is to pay off the highest interest rate debt first (Important and immediate debt), while making minimum payments to the lower interest rate debts (Secondary debt). After the highest rate debt is fully paid off, begin making larger payments on the next highest interest rate debt while still making minimum payments on the lower interest rate debts. Continue this process until all of the debts have been paid off.

A little at a time!

STEP 6
Managing payments

Once you have organized your household budget schedule, the key to staying on top of your payment plans is staying in control and finding the cheapest and most suitable way to pay as many debts as possible when your income arrives either weekly or monthly.

Choose a method that is less time consuming, if you receive your income on a weekly basis, divide all bills by 52 weeks and deposit a weekly amount into a bank account for all your categories. You can then decide to pay either weekly or monthly depending on the frequency of your income.

For example, Lucy's total income is 2,140 Euros. She receives the total amount via various sources (see step 1), she has decided to work with a monthly schedule.

	Lucy's Income		
Actual Income	**2,140**	**Monthly**	
Actual rent	550	Monthly	
Electricity	120	Bi Monthly	60Euros Monthly
Water	20	Monthly	
Phone & Internet	40	Monthly	
Transportation	80	Monthly	
Food Groceries	85	Bi weekly	170Euros Monthly
Dinning out/ Entertainment	40	Bi weekly	80Euros Monthly
Clothing/Personal	80	Monthly	
Household			

supplies	20	Monthly	
Debt pay off	300	Monthly	
Miscellaneous	140	Monthly	
Big Expense	200	Monthly	
Education costs	200	Monthly	
Total expenses	**1,940**	**Monthly**	
Savings (Money remaining from income)	200	Monthly	

Every month regardless of when Lucy expects her bills to be paid she deposits a monthly budget of all her expenses in an assigned account with the names of her categories of expenditure. On the 30th of the month her salary from her job comes in. Her child maintenance payments are scheduled to arrive on the same date. She planned her budget in a way that when her child benefit arrives, it goes straight into her income account. She collects the child benefit every week for 4 weeks, so that by the end of the month she has a total of 240 Euros in her income account.

As soon as 2,140 Euros has been completed, she knows that on the first of every month she has to pay rent. Lucy has a rent account, where she transfers her rent payment. With this method, her rent is already in the account before the first of the Month ready for transfer to her landlord.
Her electricity bill is to be paid bi monthly, so she sends 60 Euros to her sub account until she completes the next month's 60 Euros and pays for her bill in 2 months. During the summer season, she will continue to deposit the same amount in the account to assist with fluctuations in bill expenses. The same goes for all the other categories in the budget plan.

On the weeks that she has budgeted to go out, she will use the account meant for dinning out / entertainment. If she does not go out in a month, the money stays in the account and she will continue to deposit into the account on a monthly basis. This way she will still be saving by default for fun nights for herself and her kids. Budget planning is not meant to deprive the household from having a social life.

Bear in mind, everyone's priorities are different and this list can be adjusted to suit household needs and priorities. For households that take care of relatives abroad or have other commitments like building a house in their native countries, a category needs to be named to provide for this expense.

It will be easy to know in advance if a payment will be missed and it is a good idea to inform creditors in advance. Provide a statement letter stating that a payment will be missed and include how long it might last and why the missed payment will occur. Provide an offer of spreading the arrears with the current payment plan. Most times, if you have been consistent with your deposits in all the various categories, you can always shuffle and pay before it becomes an issue and return the money back to the category you borrowed from.

This will require discipline….A lot of discipline!

Here is an example of a monthly budget plan temple. You can also prepare an excel sheet and prepare a customized category to suit your household needs and expenses.

Household Monthly Budget

Date

	Budget	Actual	Planned
Income			
Salary 1			
Salary 2			
Benefits			
Other Income			
Total Income			
Expenses			
Fixed Costs			
Mortgage / Rent Expense			
Car / Hire purchase Payment(s)			
Loan Payment(s)			
Insurance - Car			
Insurance - Homeowner's			
Insurance - Life			
Tithe			
Childcare/Education			
Vacations			
Care for relatives			
Total Costs			
Secondary Costs			
Electric / Gas Expense			
Telephone Expense			
Cable / Satellite Television Expense			
Internet Expense			

Food (Groceries)			
Gasoline			
Pet Supplies			
Medical / Healthcare			
Personal Care			
Food (Dining Out & Entertainment)			
Other Secondary Costs			
Total Secondary Costs			
Entertainment			
Gifts			
Clothing			
Miscellaneous			
Other Costs			
Other Costs			
Total Costs			
Total Expenses			
Savings			

STEP 7
Evaluating budgets regularly

If you find that your actual spending varies a lot from your budget, you will have to readjust the figures in your budget to make it more realistic. In this case, go back to Step 2 and reduce some expenses, or restrict your spending in some categories.

If your actual spending varies only a little from your budget, you are on the right track.

If you are not saving enough or are not able to pay off your debts, find other ways to cut down on expenses and adjust your budget accordingly.

Keep up the good work! If you can stick to your budget closely, you should find that your income covers your expenses and that you are saving enough for your financial goals.

Evaluating your budget means looking at your past expenses and creating an improved version that reflects your financial goals. A balanced budget is when income exceeds expenses—that is, you are able to save a bit of money each week or month. This is the ideal scenario. Your budget is what will guide your spending in future months and help you save money.

- Use Step 3 to guide you, but adjust the figures as you go along, while you think of the following:
    o Do the figures in my budget reflect my expenses in *any* given month? If not, what would be a more realistic figure?
    o Are there any small, recurring expenses that I can cut?
    o Are there expenses in the secondary categories that I can cut?

- Do I want to add money to certain new spending categories that reflect my financial goals, such as saving for a holiday or creating an emergency fund?
- Are the differences between my actual spending and my planned budget large or small?
- In which categories are the differences the largest? Why? Is it because of an unusual situation or is this likely to happen each month?
- Am I able to save enough money to reach my financial goals or to pay off my debts?

Once you are done, take total income and deduct total expenses to find out how much money you will be able to save. Adjust your expenses where you can so that your monthly savings help you meet your goals for the future.

STEP 8
Setting financial goals

A very important part of making your budget work for you is to decide what you want to achieve. If money were no object, what would you and your family members like to be doing? Think about what is important for you, what are you trying to achieve in the next five to ten years?

Brainstorm with your family about family goals. At the brainstorming phase write down any goals or dreams that your family would like to achieve. Then estimate how much it would cost, and note an amount next to it.

Now that you have all the things that you would love to purchase on a list, prioritize them by importance, and assign a realistic date by when you would like to accomplish them. Next, group them under these categories:

Short-term goals can be accomplished within two years.

Mid-term goals can be accomplished within two to five years.

Long-term financial goals may take more than five years to accomplish

Your objective is to reach your goals without getting in debt; therefore you have to plan regular savings that are aimed specifically to each goal. Make sure you keep your goals realistic and flexible. Don't set them too high, or it would just get frustrating.

STEP 9
Dealing with a spendthrift partner

Managing finances can sometimes seem like a difficult task. This difficulty is sometimes compounded when you have to deal with a **partner** that likes to **spend** money. Here are a few tips for managing your finances when you have to live with someone that does not like to save.

Saving With Partners

When trying to implement a budget with a partner, it can often feel like you are trying to impose your will upon them. If the partner does not see how saving can benefit them, then they are not likely to go through with the plan. They will be much more likely to help you save if you can show them what is in it for them. Talk to them about what they want. Find out their hopes and dreams (Refer to step 8). If you can agree upon a common goal, it will be much easier to get them to work with you. For example, show them that if you save a certain amount of money each month, you can take a nice holiday. Anything that they can visualize will help this process. Talk to them in terms of end results and it will help justify short-term sacrifices.

Pocket Money

Another strategy that you could utilize is giving them an allowance. If you are in charge of the money, you can provide them with a certain amount of money each pay period. Let them know that they are free to use the money as they wish. However, once the money runs out, there will not be any more available until the next payday. This may take some convincing in order to get them to agree to this plan. However, if you are both working towards a common goal, and they understand that they have problems controlling money, they will be more likely to agree. This also provides them with a certain amount of freedom in their spending. When we do not allow our partner to spend any money, they will often get discouraged. Giving them a certain amount of money each pay period will keep their spirits up and make it much more likely for them to follow through.

Shopping Online

Another problem that couples often have is they allow the person that spends the most money to go out to do the shopping. If one partner is not good at handling money, it will be helpful for the household to organize their shopping online. If you want to make sure that your budget is adhered to, you need to be there to oversee the process. Each person in the couple should focus on their strengths and what they bring to the relationship. This can help you stick to the budget and avoid personal problems along the way.

- Meals away from home are a major drain on resources, and your partner may not even realize how much they spend on food. Send him or her to work with a home-made lunch.
- Desperate times call for desperate measures-put those credit cards on ice! If they can't make it into your partner's wallet, they can't be used.
- Teach your partner the joy and necessity of saving for a rainy day. Set saving goals that both of you can attain together, and plan rewards for staying on target.
- Control purchases made on a whim, the best way to do this is to ask your partner to wait a day or two before making a major purchase so that a rational decision can be made.
- It is better to maintain separate accounts, with a limited balance to avoid overspending.
- It is just not going to work if you try to control your partner's spending, but YOU still go on spending sprees. Show your partner how to be economical by limiting YOUR expenses.
- Tally up your partner's giddy expenses and ask them to consider what else could have been bought with that money: a well-earned holiday, down payment on a home, or even a car.
- It is worth just a Euro or two, so it doesn't matter that your partner bought something totally unnecessary, right? Wrong! It is the small molehills that add up to form a mountain of debt. Control your partner's unwarranted spending, even if it is just a small amount.

- Make sure you are both paying for purchases only with cash. This will restrict the amount of money you both have on hand.

- If your partner has a spending problem, It's **OKAY** to ask where all of the money goes. Once your partner realizes they'll have to account for every single cent spent, frivolous spending should go down.

- Sales, bargains, and discounts are tempting, but when you are spending money unnecessarily, it doesn't matter what a deal it is.

- If your partner is unhappy, he or she could be compensating with compulsive spending. Try cheering your partner up and see the change.

- Lay down the spending rules with an authoritative air. Sometimes, that's the only way to make sure your partner learns good money habits.

- Encourage your partner to go window shopping, leaving money at home. It is an imaginary purchase exercise that provides a fair amount of pleasure at no cost.

- Sometimes, it's better to be understanding and help them through the problem instead of ranting and raving every time your partner spends some money.

- If your normally spendthrift partner has been good for a while, don't rejoice too soon. Compulsive spenders can relapse any moment, just like drug or alcohol addicts. Watch out for this pattern and continue to be supportive.

In extreme cases where it is impossible to work with your spouse/partner then the bulk of the planning may fall on you – do not despair (as noted everyone's case is different); look for extra places to increase your income in order to manage your bills.

Remember that contracts you do not sign you are not responsible for!

Stick to bills that affect you directly in order to avoid debt problems/bad credit rating.

STEP 10
Holding everyone accountable

Ultimately, your best efforts will only save you money and keep your finances in line if your entire household is on board. You will need to make sure they are aware of the budget and are doing their best to stick to it. This is a great way to teach children about the importance of budgeting, involve them in the discussion and show them why saving or investing is important. By holding others accountable, you may even find you are additionally more accountable to your own budget.

Conclusion

Managing household finances is an extremely difficult task to adhere to. It requires discipline and the support of all members within the household. I have worked on managing household finances for the past ten years with a lot of ups and downs.

I also understand the mental and emotional headaches that go with it. When all individuals in the household are not on board, it becomes more difficult to manage.

This was why I added a step on *"Dealing with a spendthrift partner"*. When there is no cooperation between partners in a household, paying off debts, keeping on top of household budgets can be a stressful and daunting task. Creditors pounding on doors with threat letters and court orders, make the whole budget *thing* even more alarming.

I hope that the ten steps given in this book will enable a less daunting move towards a stress free way of managing household budgets.

Made in the USA
Charleston, SC
15 October 2013